HOW TO MAKE

£1,000 PER WEEK

RUNNING YOUR

OWN UNIQUE

MARKETING

BUSINESS

By Ray Fox, B.SC., FCIS, Principal, The Bottom Line Consultancy

First Edition published in 2015 by The Bottom Line Consultancy

Hurst Cottage, Bottle Square Lane, Radnage,

Buckinghamshire. HP14 4DP, United Kingdom

Tel: 01494 483728 Fax: 01494 484039

Email: fox@estelle-alan.com

Ray Fox has asserted his right to be identified as the author of this work in accordance with sections 77 and 78 of the Copyright, Designs and Patents Act 1988.

ISBN-13: 978-1511693912
ISBN-10: 1511693916

First edition 2015

Printed and bound by Amazon Creates

NOTE: The material contained in this book is set out in good faith for general guidance and no liability can be accepted for loss or expense incurred as a result of relying in particular circumstances on statements made in this book. Laws and regulations are complex and liable to change, and readers should check the current positions with the relevant authorities in their country of origin before making personal arrangements.

This book is available online and at all good bookstores.

THE PHILOSOPHY OF RUNNING YOUR OWN BUSINESS

There are no short cuts to success. Regardless of what anyone tells you, there are no get rich quick schemes. If somebody promises you that you do nothing but that the money keeps rolling in, grab your money and run in the opposite direction as fast as your legs can carry you. As the old saying goes, when a man with money meets a man with experience, the man with money is going to get some experience and the man with experience will get some of the money!

There is only one true route to success in this world. Firstly, you have to decide what it is you want to achieve. Secondly, get started. Thirdly, do not stop until you achieve what you set out to achieve. Persistence and determination are omnipotent.

However, why start from scratch? Many of the great secrets of business success have already been discovered. All you need to do is find a system that works for others and improve upon it. Why re-invent the wheel? If you truly want financial success and security, you need a vehicle ~ a proven business idea that works. Read on and you will find out what the vehicle is and how it works.

Contents Page

INTRODUCTION

When I set up my first company, I was told that it was easy to make £1,000,000. You did not necessarily have to come up with a new idea but you should take an existing idea, one that works, and improve it by 10%.

At its simplest level, most businesses buy a product or offer a service for, say £X and then sell it for, say, £X plus 50%. Providing the cost of sales and distribution, etc. is less than the 50%, you make money. If you get others to do the selling for you, you make even more money.

Our business concept is absolutely unique. It does not rely on buying a product at one price and selling it at another price. It revolves around the fact that there are businesses that are already selling products and services and want to sell more of those products and services. How do you know that these businesses want to increase their sales? Well, they tell you. How do they tell you? Well, they advertise in Yellow Pages, Thomson Directories, local directories, on the Internet and in other publications. They advertise in newspapers and magazines. They advertise on the radio and in newsagents' windows. They put their names and addresses on the sides of their vehicles. They arrange for leaflets to be put through your doors. They advertise through direct mail. Some have even tried bulk faxing. Others use bulk email. Some sponsor sports events. Others market using mobile phone text messages. Many organisations sell over the telephone. Any company that goes to the trouble and expense of advertising is doing it for only one reason. They want to increase their sales. These Companies are your potential customers. You don't even have to go far to find them as they are all listed in your local telephone directories.

Hopefully, I have convinced you that the market place is virtually limitless. The next thing you have to understand is that it does not really matter where you live to be able to operate this business effectively. Wherever there are shops, stores, high streets, town centres or shopping malls, you will find companies and people. People and companies who want to sell their products and services and people who want to buy products and services. So you see, you might live in the centre of London or you might live in the tiniest village, the principle holds true regardless. That is the secret of this marketing business. In essence, it is like being a marriage broker only instead of bringing couples together to get married, you will be bringing people together who want to do business together. In simple terms, a buyer and a seller. The truly fun part of this is that you can make a fortune on the way if you follow the ideas we will be giving you.

As mentioned above, the path to success has already been well mapped out for you because we have already made the mistakes in the past and eliminated them. We will not tell you what does not work. We will only tell you what does work. A tried and tested formula. Simple to understand and easy to follow.

Why should we release these secrets to you? Quite simply, there are over 70 million people in the UK alone. Hundreds of millions of people in the EU and the rest of Europe. Hundreds of millions of people in the USA and Canada. Hundreds of millions of people in Australasia, Asia, the Middle East, South America and Africa. This idea is so simple that it can work in any area, any province, any state, any country, any continent. We already have a successful business with more opportunities than we could ever have dreamed of. So we offer this idea to you at a nominal cost and to give you the opportunity to be successful yourself. We are so unlikely to be competitors that it does not really matter. Even if we were, there is more than enough business around the world that if another thousand times as many people became involved in an identical business, between us, we still would not scratch the surface of the potential revenue opportunities.

In the following pages, you will find everything you need to make this business a success. You can grow it on a part-time or full-time basis. As your business grows, it is limited only by the size of your own imagination.

Because it is your own business, you can run it entirely yourself. You can use third parties to handle the design and print work. Alternatively, you can use graphics and images from Google as the basis for the design or you can make your own using a package like Power Point or Photo Shop. In the appendix, you will find draft layouts for the type of product you will be marketing. All you need to do is have your own designs made, get them printed and distributed. You can even get commission sales agents to do the selling for you. The business then runs itself and all you have to do is co-ordinate the activities and count the money as it comes in.

THE BUSINESS CONCEPT

We call this business the "Cheque Book Voucher" method of marketing, and, as explained, the concept is remarkably simple. To begin with, think for a moment of the main methods that local businesses bring their products and services to the attention of potential purchasers. When you think of it, there are really only a handful of possible ways.

Local Directories

We are all familiar with the main directories such as Yellow Pages and Thomson Directories. But there are many more in the market place. Trade Directories, Newsletters, the Internet, Chamber of Commerce Directories, etc. Almost every local business has an entry in one directory or another. Just a quick flick through them and you will see pages packed with advertisements. Let's suppose that you were a local consumer and you want to find a local product or service. Who do you choose and why? Imagine that you want to pick an accountant [let's face it, when this business gets off the ground properly, you are going to be needing one pretty quickly]. You look in the local directory or on the Internet. You have to find the right category for Accountants. When you find the right category, you are then faced with, maybe, 20, 30 or even

40 Accountants all offering the same or similar services. How do you decide which one to choose? The one with the biggest advert? The first one in the directory? The last one in the directory? The one with a familiar sounding name? Think for a moment what you would do if *you* were the accountant. What would you do to get *your* advertisement noticed? Perhaps spend a small fortune on a large and distinctive advert to be noticed. The other major drawback to directories is that they are generally only printed once a year. If you were a new business, you would have to wait a whole year before you got your entry in. What would you do if you have a special offer, say an autumn sale or a Christmas special ~ how could a directory help you here?

Local Newspapers

Local newspapers certainly have a part to play in local advertising. Some of them are paid for and some of them are free. If you buy a newspaper, the likelihood is that you want to read it rather than look at the adverts. On the other hand, the newspapers are so packed with adverts that we do not tend to pay any attention to them. Added to this is the fact that the majority of local newspapers are bought on a Friday, glimpsed at over the weekend and thrown away by Monday morning. Going back to our scenario earlier, if you were the Accountant wanting to attract our attention, you would have to place large enough adverts to get noticed, place them every week at the same time praying that your potential customer won't be looking for an accountant between Monday and Friday, when all your advert will be doing is wrapping up somebody's fish and chips.

So what other options are there to attract local customers to local businesses? Well, you could try a leaflet drop ~ but it's very expensive and incredibly hit and miss. You could try direct mail. Again, it's very expensive. You could try the newsagents' windows but this looks incredibly amateurish.

What you need is a professional, yet inexpensive way of bringing the local business's products and services to the attention of local customers in such a way that is friendly, cost effective, likely to be retained and isn't full of competitive adverts. The Cheque Book Voucher form of advertising is the answer.

The Product

We are all familiar with a chequebook. Although it doesn't really need any explanation, a standard chequebook will have, say, thirty cheques in it and the only difference between each cheque is the cheque number. Imagine thirty adverts, money off coupons, special offers, etc. all bound together in the form of a chequebook. In this sense, each chequebook would be the same but would have, say, thirty offers in each one. All you have to do is to find thirty local businesses that each want to target their products and services to a specific local area. You take their orders, get a printer to design and print, say, 15,000 copies and arrange with a local leaflet distribution company to have them delivered. Each household will receive a free of charge chequebook full of promotional offers. They won't throw them away because they'll never know when they'll need them and none of the adverts will be from competitive businesses so there won't be the difficulties experienced in the local directories with the consumer having to choose between competitive services.

Advantages of the cheque book vouchers

For a start, the chequebooks can be specifically targeted to a particular geographical area where all the recipients are potential customers for the products and services being offered. Because not all of the offers are likely to be used at once, the likelihood is that the recipient will keep the chequebook handy for when they do need a particular service. There is exclusive advertising for a particular line of business. The concept can be repeated in different geographical areas on a rotating basis, returning to a previously targeted area, say, every three months. Perhaps the most exciting advantage of the chequebook voucher is that the whole idea is unbelievably profitable.

Profit Analysis

Let's assume that you sell, on average, to 30 customers per month. That's only one each day so that should be easily achievable. Each sale produces a revenue of £300. Total sales of £9,000. Your only expenses are artwork, design and printing of the 15,000 chequebooks. Let's say this costs £4,000. Then you have to get them distributed. Let's say this costs £1,000. That leaves you with total expenses of £5,000 ~ a net profit of £4,000. Not bad for one month's work!! Remember, this is only one project, in one specific area. For the next two months, you can do different areas and perhaps come back to the first area again.

This time, your potential customers will have had, hopefully, a significant response to the earlier cheque book and would now like the same advert placed in another cheque book in a different area. The whole concept can be infinitely expanded covering as many areas as you wish to target. Now you can see why we are not likely to be competitors.

The intention of the above is to give you an idea for the concept and the potential profit you can earn.

Who are your customers?

As we have said previously, any business selling a product or service in a particular area and who would be interested in selling more of that product or service to a local household is a potential customer.

You will find them listed in the directories mentioned above, the local newspapers, leaflet drops, newsagents' windows and on the side of vans. Within these categories, you will find literally tens of thousands of potential customers for the chequebook voucher.

How do you approach them?

To a certain extent, this is something that, at the beginning, you will be doing [unless you have sales staff to do it for you] and so you will have to be comfortable with the approach. There are various ways of targeting new business. Telephoning is probably the most effective way of getting the business off the ground quickly. It is relatively cheap, especially as you will be making local calls. Some of the new telephone systems offer free local calls. Some of the mobile providers offer free calls and Skype calls are incredibly cheap to make. It is unlikely that you will complete many sales on the telephone but it should lead you to appointments with the prospect of a subsequent face-to-face sale. Another option is face-to-face selling. This is relatively easy to do when your potential prospects are in the same geographical area. In fact, if you take a typical high street, you could probably go down one side and up the other side and sell to each shop on the way. You could also try direct mail. When you do your first print-run, arrange to have an extra 1,000 or so produced. These could be sent out with a direct mail letter to each of your potential prospects. You would then need to follow up with a phone call and subsequent appointment but at least the prospect will have seen the finished product.

Don't be afraid of selling the product. Every prospect you meet spends hour after hour, day after day, trying to work out new ways of bringing their products and services to the attention of customers. If you have something new and novel and that certainly works, many will give you a try. Remember, you only have to make one sale per day to earn £4,000 per month so concentrate on the benefits, not on the difficulties, of selling. You could always sub-contract out the selling and pay a commission based on performance to a number of sales personnel.

The advantages of self-employment

1. You are your own boss. You work when you like for as long as you like. During the day, in the evenings, at weekends, in the middle of the night if that is what suits you!!

2. You require little or no capital expenditure. A functional computer, a desk, chair, some letter headed paper and a small amount of space and you are in business. This business could easily be run from a garage, a shed, a spare bedroom or even the dining room or kitchen table.

    An inexpensive computer, printer, monitor, answer phone and fax machine can all be bought for less than a couple of hundred pounds.

3. The overheads are minimal. This business can easily be run from home. You definitely do not require purpose built offices with 21st Century equipment. When your business grows, you may be inclined to purchase these. At the beginning, your primary expenses are letter-headed paper, envelopes, postage, broadband plus the occasional telephone call or fax.

4. You do not need any expensive staff to employ. The whole

concept behind our cheque book voucher marketing system of running a business is that it can be run by yourself, or, of course, by a couple. But you do not need to employ anybody.

5. You will not need any major capital injection to purchase stock.

6. As you will not be buying stock, you will not need a large area for the storage of products. This again, cuts down on the overheads.

7. You do not need any technical knowledge about the products being advertised by your customers. Your role is purely and simply to take your customers' orders and then get the Cheque Book Vouchers designed, printed and distributed.

8. You do not require any specialised marketing experience. As we have said earlier, your role is purely and simply to introduce the concept to your prospects.

9. Earnings from this system will probably continue for many years. Most of the customers that you sell to once will come back time after time for repeated inclusions in future cheque books. Once a relationship has been formed, your income will continue with little or no effort on

your part for many years to come.

10. There is no lack of potential customers who want you to try and increase the sales of their products and services for them. Similarly, although it is self-evident, there is no lack of geographical areas that their products and services can be targeted at.

11. For these reasons, your earnings potential is, virtually, limitless. You can handle as many customers in as many areas and with whatever frequency of distribution as you want to. The only limit is how hard you want to work and how much money you want to make.

12. There are no Government regulations that can cause you any concern, apart from the possible need to register for VAT when your turnover reaches the appropriate level. Your Accountant can handle this.

13. Finally, and perhaps most importantly, this system we have developed allows you to tap in to all the directories, newspapers and local advertising free of charge. In other words, somebody else has already done the work for you to identify who your potential customers are. All you have to do is talk to them.

STARTING UP IN BUSINESS

Your Office

You do not need expensive or elaborate office space to start up your business. If need be, you could start off by running your business from the kitchen or dining room table or spare bedroom.

Your minimal requirement consists of a desk and a chair, some filing and shelf space, a computer, printer and a telephone. If these are not readily available, the small ads in your local newspaper or a visit to a local boot fair will invariably lead you to second-hand equipment at reasonable prices.

If you have a spare room, it could easily be converted into an office. If not, perhaps a corner of the garage, bedroom or loft will suffice. Wherever you can work quietly and not be disturbed, nor disturb others, is good enough.

Your trading image

Your image to your potential customers, in the first instance at least, depends on what you think of yourself as well as what others think of you. At the beginning, you will be dealing with manufacturers, retail outlets, shops, suppliers of professional services, etc. You are not going to be inviting them into your home so they will not know that your business is being run from, say, your kitchen table. Consequently, you must give them the impression that you are a BIG company and that can only be done by giving the impression that you are a big company. The following will give the people you are dealing with the impression that you are a big company.

[a] Facsimile

Every big company has a facsimile number. A fax provides instant transmission of documents down the telephone. In the business world, a fax is as common as a telephone. Without one, you will appear very small and amateurish. In the UK, they are becoming incredibly cheap. One can be purchased new with a built in telephone and answer phone for under a hundred pounds. Second hand ones are even cheaper. Some can be linked to an existing phone system so that you do not even need an extra phone line installed. The great advantage of fax is that drawings and pictures can be sent and the transmission is instantaneous. Your faxes can even be sent in the evenings when the calls are much cheaper. If you cannot afford a fax, you can obtain a shared facility through the local Chamber of Commerce or a local shared office facility. Details can be found in your local Yellow Pages or Thomson Directory. If you have the appropriate computer equipment fitted with broadband, it is possible to use your computer to transmit scanned copies of your drawings and pictures.

Make sure you show your fax number, email address and web site on your letter headed paper and business cards and encourage people to use email as letters can take days to arrive even when posted locally.

[b] Electronic Mail

If you have the computer technology and the desire to link into the Internet, then this is obviously for you. For further information, contact your local computer shop. Many I T consultants advertise in the local newspapers and you could easily do a barter deal with one of them – they set up your I T system for you in exchange for free advertising.

[c] Professional Qualifications

Some people have been to University and College ~ others have not. Education is not a prerequisite to success in our line of business but your image will be greatly enhanced if you have letters after your name. Just ask yourself, what is more impressive: Bill Bloggs or Bill Bloggs, M.Bar., M.MAA., M.Inst.SMM., CIF. These "qualifications" (and there are many others) can be obtained by applying for membership of the British Agents Register (Harrogate 60608), The Manufacturers Agents Association (Reigate 43492), The Institute of Sales and Marketing Management (Luton 411130) and The International Society of Financiers, (call the USA, +1.704.252.5907).

[d] Professional Organisations

In addition to your professional qualifications, once your business is off and running, you may well consider joining some of the professional organisations such as The British Institute of Management [Corby and London], The Institute of Directors [London], The Institute of Export [London], The Federation of Small Businesses [London] and The National Association of the Self Employed [London].

You would also be well advised to join your local Chamber of Commerce as well as other professional business groups in your area as these will widen your sphere of business and professional contacts. You should also subscribe to *World Money Exchange*, which is one of the main networking organisations (01494.483728). As a buyer of this book, you will be entitled to a discount off the annual subscription.

[e] Letter-headed paper

As we have stated previously, your image is what others think of you. Consequently, it is important that you use quality letter headed paper with matching envelopes where possible. Try and have your address printed on your envelopes so that any mail that is undelivered will be returned to you. In the short term, particularly until your business is profitable, you may consider using a rubber stamp showing your address that you can put on the reverse of your envelopes. A local printer or stationer can do this for under £10. You could also have small labels printed. These only cost about £5 for 1,000. These printers can also produce a customised logo to appear on your letterhead, business cards and envelopes.

[f] Trading Style

Your image improves with a good trading style. Bloggs Marketing, BB Trading, BB Commercial, Bloggs Enterprises, Bloggs Global Trading all give the impression of a large organisation. If you wish, you could form yourself into a Limited Company [contact Companies House in Cardiff 01222.388588]. You may need to get the advice of a Solicitor and/or an Accountant on the pros and cons of forming a limited company.

Whilst on the subject of professional advisers, do not forget to contact your local bank and set up a Business Account, notify your tax office as well as start to keep some form of financial records. Again, any local accountant can advise you here although we've found that QuickBooks is an incredibly simple way of keeping good accounting records and a copy can be bought from Currys/PCWorld.

If you already have a good relationship with your local bank, speak to the manager - they can normally provide you with a business start-up pack as well as put you in touch with a good local accountant.

THE SUCCESSFUL RUNNING OF YOUR MARKETING BUSINESS

As with all businesses, there are easy and hard ways of making it successful. The whole point of this manual is to teach you what we already know and save you the trouble and expense of making those same mistakes. Running your marketing business at the beginning may only be part-time when you already have a full-time job. Consequently, time is of the essence so it is best not to waste it.

Writing letters can be a daunting task especially if everyone has to be done individually. One way of short-circuiting the typing of letters is to type out a standard letter and then have it printed or photocopied onto your own letter-headed paper. All you will need to do then is to type in a personalised address in the blank spaces. The recipient will never know that you have not sent a personal letter.

If you have the resources, buy a small computer and printer. Second-hand machines only cost a couple of hundred pounds and then you have your own word-processing capability. If you cannot afford this, a local word-processing bureau will do this for you for a couple of pence a letter.

It is essential that you keep your filing constantly up to date. You will regularly make hundreds of contacts with prospective customers, printers and leaflet distribution companies. It is essential that you keep some form of cross-referenced filing system showing prospective customers, printers, leaflet distribution companies, etc. in each area you are working in. Cheap filing cabinets can be obtained from a second-hand office furniture dealer or through the small ads. Another essential requirement is a telephone answering machine. If you are working in a full time job during the day, your calls must be taken. With some answer phones, it is possible to listen to your messages by ringing from another number.

EXPANDING YOUR BUSINESS

Going full time in your business may have been your original intention right from the start. However, do not let you dream of running your own full-time business become a nightmare that ends up running you.

This is a very important decision and one that you should only take after you have discussed this with your spouse (if applicable), your Accountant and your Lawyer.

As your full-time employment still produces a salary, use the money earned from this business to modernise your office whilst living on the income of your job. Purchase the necessary time saving equipment that will help make running the business easier. If you do not need the equipment, put the money you earn from your full-time job into the bank or building society and live only on the money you earn from the business. After six or nine months, you will see whether your earnings from the business support you sufficiently. Then, and only then, resign from you full-time job.

What else will you need to know?

Having taken orders from customers, make sure they pay you in advance. Your potential cost of printing is quite high so you cannot put your customers on credit terms. Offer them a 2% discount for immediate payment but allowing credit will only increase your expenses and minimise your profits. Most major printers should be able to handle the artwork, design and printing of the chequebook vouchers ready for distribution. These can found on the high street, such as Pronto print, PDC Copy print and many more. If you don't have one nearby, just check them out in your local directory.

The same applies for leaflet distribution companies. Many of the local newspapers will provide a leaflet distribution service but you have to check that they are reliable. It wouldn't be unknown for certain quantities of the leaflets not to reach the intended destination. Check what quality procedures are in place to ensure that the chequebooks actually arrive where they are supposed to. When using a leaflet distribution company for the first time, it may be worth your while knocking on a couple of doors in the area to check that the chequebooks have actually been delivered.

Finally, let us wish you well. This business works and a substantial full or part-time income can be produced with effort, enthusiasm and perseverance. Good luck.

APPENDIX

Exhibit 1

YOUR FREE CHEQUEBOOK OF PROMOTIONAL VOUCHERS

Exhibit 2

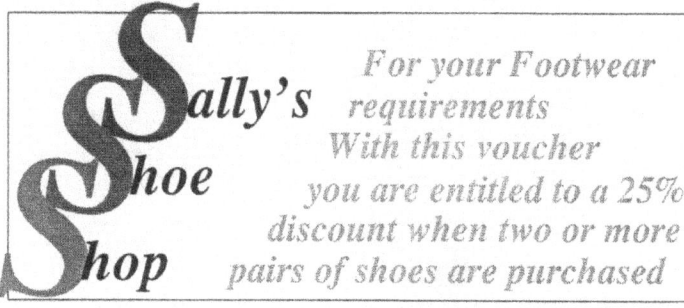

For your Footwear requirements With this voucher you are entitled to a 25% discount when two or more pairs of shoes are purchased

ACCOUNTANTS

Let us balance your books

small businesses and the self employed are our speciality

PROFIT & LOSS

THE COMPUTER CENTRE
FOR ALL YOUR PC, PRINTER, FAX & SOFTWARE NEEDS

THIS VOUCHER ENTITLES YOU TO A DISCOUNT OF
20% WHEN YOU SPENT £250 OR MORE

Exhibit 3

Wedding & Portrait photography
a speciality

PHIL'S PH TOGRAPHICS

25% off on production
of this voucher

Wildes
Windows
FOR WINDOWS,
DOORS AND CONSERVATORIES
**10% OFF ON PRODUCTION
OF THIS VOUCHER**

FOR ALL THE LATEST FILMS **£1 OFF** ALL RENTALS WITH THIS VOUCHER	FOR ALL THE LATEST FILMS **£1 OFF** ALL RENTALS WITH THIS VOUCHER	FOR ALL THE LATEST FILMS **£1 OFF** ALL RENTALS WITH THIS VOUCHER
MONDAY	TUESDAY	WEDNESDAY

Exhibit 4

Exhibit 5

ed's auto emporium

for MOT's crash repairs and all servicing

FREE MOT

with every full service with this voucher

THE ESTATE AGENCY

SOLD

Let us sell your house or flat 12% discount on all sole agency clients who produce this voucher on completion

THE LOOSE WIRE

15% DISCOUNT
FOR ALL YOUR
ELECTRICAL NEEDS
ON PRODUCTION OF
THIS VOUCHER

Exhibit 6

Exhibit 7

Exhibit 8

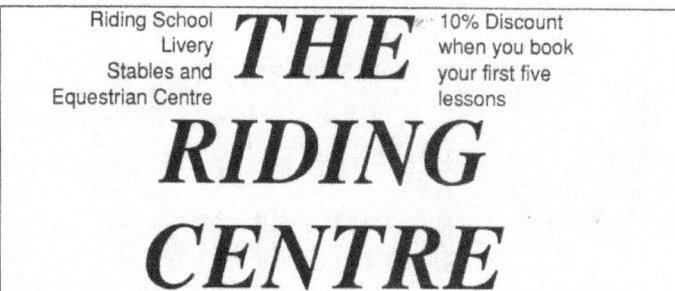

Exhibit 9

Exhibit 10

Exhibit 11

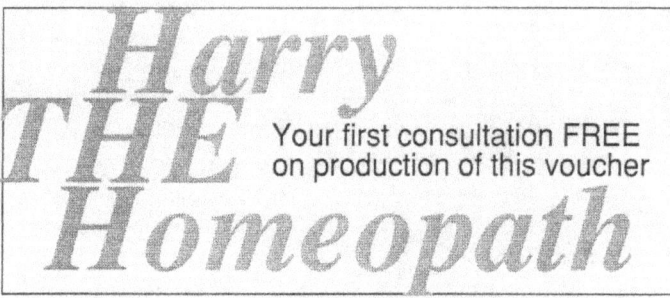

ABOUT THE AUTHOR
Ray Fox

Ray Fox is sixty-one years of age. He originally qualified with a B.Sc. (Hons.) degree in Behavioural Science (specialising in Industrial Psychology and Human Behaviour) from the University of Aston in Birmingham.

After graduation, he studied for and completed the examinations for The Institute of Chartered Secretaries and Administrators. He is a Fellow of the Institute (FCIS). Following that, he studied for and obtained a Diploma in Company Law and a Diploma in Company Secretarial Practice from the School of Accountancy and Business Studies.

For eight and a half years [from 1979 until 1987], Ray was the Company Secretary of a £50m turnover engineering company. In 1987 he joined Dun & Bradstreet, a US$3B turnover company, as their UK Company Secretary. Over the subsequent seven years, he was promoted to Company Secretary of D & B Europe, then the D & B Group and was subsequently appointed as their UK Director of Legal and Pensions Services. He was also Company Secretary of D & B Group's Pension Plan responsible for all administration and £100M of Pension Fund investments. Ray left D & B in 1994 to set up his own Consulting Practice.

For over twenty years, he has been running a very successful marketing consultancy specialising in the Legal profession. To date, he has worked with over 685 Solicitors' Practices, Law Firms, Patent Agents and Licensed Conveyancers, both in the UK and overseas. His support for the Legal profession has tended to fall into one of four broad categories:

1. Helping them generate more Clients

2. Helping them sell, merge or value their Practices

3. Helping them acquire other Practices

4. Helping them with P I insurance and staff recruitment

He has worked for over 300 Solicitors' practices helping them generate more Commercial Clients.

In addition to the above, he is one of the Founder Members and a Director of Core Legal, [see www.CoreLegal.net] which is a networking organisation of professional companies all of whom provide specialist support to the legal profession. He was also a General Commissioner of Taxes and one of the Co-Authors of "Running a Successful Law Firm – Strategies and Tips for Success".

He is active in Freemasonry, having been Worshipful Master of a number of Lodges and is also a member of The Worshipful Company of Chartered Secretaries and Administrators, one of the modern Livery Companies of the City of London.

Ray is also the brains behind a number of highly successful web sites:

www.BottomLineConsultancy.com

www.SolicitorSupermarket.biz

www.RecruitmentForSolicitors.co.uk

www.NEDexchange.co.uk

www.ProfessionalDirectors.co.uk

www.YourEnglishOffice.com

www.YourAmericanOffice.biz

www.TradeAndFinanceDiploma.com

www.StopTheTaxMan.com

www.WorldMoneyExchange.co.uk

www.Estelle-Alan-Group.com

www.EstelleAlanPublications.com

www.CompanyFormationCorporation.com

www.InsuranceForSolicitors.co.uk

www.UKTradeAdvisoryServices.com

www.YourOffshoreBankAccount.biz

OTHER BOOKS BY THE AUTHOR

More Commercial Clients And How To Get Them

A 'How To' Book for Solicitors' Practices
Published: 2014

ISBN: 978-1505488715

I know we don't want to admit it or say the words out loud but here goes – "Generally, Solicitors are crap at marketing". There, I've said it. We all know it's true but what can we do about it? A lot of Solicitors' Practices will spend a lot of money on marketing, but this doesn't often pick up more commercial clients - a group who are often more profitable than a typical private client. This book is about how to get more commercial clients.

How To Make £1000 Per Week Running Your Own Import / Export Agency

Published: 2015

ISBN: 978-1507722176

Have you ever thought about running your own import / export business? Do you want to know what to do and how to go about it? This handy little book contains tips, the steps, letter and agency contract templates, which you can amend and use for your own purpose. It is absolutely possible to make £1,000 Per Week Running Your Own Import / Export Agency from home.

OTHER BOOKS WHICH MIGHT BE OF INTEREST

Running A Successful Law Firm
Strategies & Tips for Success
Published: 2014

ISBN: 978-1492870890

Corelegal specialise in working with solicitors / lawyers. Between the contributing authors there is over 100 years collective experience. This book aims to bring that knowledge to you – giving you

fresh ideas and perspective. Avoid the expensive, painful and time consuming mistakes that most solicitors make and make your law firm a profitable success!

Constant Cashflow
How to Make Money Flow To You Every Single Day
Published: 2014

ISBN: 978-1 500601225

The problem with 'Cashflow' is that often businesses and individuals are too reliant on just one income stream/ source. Instead of just having 'one/two' jobs or key clients, and 'twenty' expenses, why not turn this around? What this book promotes is that everyday should be a payday - and it explains how and why.

Make The Most of Your Money
How to budget, save and manage your finances.

First Published: 2013

ISBN: 978-1481990639

This book looks at how to make the most of your money. Often the harder you work, the less you have to show for it. This book covers the issue of money. All the stuff you should have been taught in school including income, stocks, bonds, assets, reducing debt, mortgages, loans.

How To Write A Book In Two Weeks (or Less)

First Published: 2013

ISBN: 978-1492273554

Do you have a burning desire to write a book, but don't know how? Have you been thinking about writing a book for a while, but have just never 'gotten round to it?' Would you like to get your book completed quickly? Serial entrepreneur & author Lisa Newton explains how to write a book in two weeks (or less), which works particularly well for writing non-fiction books, business books and self-help books.

To order further copies of this book please fill in the form:

No. of copies	Title	Price	Total
	More Commercial Clients And How To Get Them	£12.50	
	How To Make £1,000 Per Week Running Your Own Import /Export Agency	£10.00	
	How To Make £1000 Per Week Running Your Own Unique Marketing Business	£10.00	
	For P&P add **£2.50** for the first book, **£1** for each extra book		
GRAND TOTAL			**£**

Name: _____

Address: _____

City: _____ Country: _____

Postcode / Zip: _____

Daytime Tel. No./Email: _____

(in case of query)

I enclose a Cheque made payable to **The Bottom Line Consultancy** for **£**
_____

Please return forms to: (Photocopies acceptable)

Direct Mail Dept., The Bottom Line Consultancy, Hurst Cottage, Bottle Square Lane, Radnage, Buckinghamshire. HP14 4DP, UK
Enquiries to: fox@estelle-alan.com

The Bottomline Consultancy (directly or via its agents) may mail, email or phone you about promotions or products. [ ] Tick box if you do not want these from us
www.BottomLineConsultancy.com

www.ingramcontent.com/pod-product-compliance
Lightning Source LLC
Chambersburg PA
CBHW071008180526
45168CB00003B/1337